Foreword

Maria Balshaw
Director, The Whitworth and Manchester City Galleries

It's all about coming together and being part of life and giving something back.
Pauline Karpidas

My introduction to Pauline Karpidas and to Hydra came courtesy of Robin Vousden, Director at Gagosian Gallery. Robin once lived in the publicly-funded museum sector and cut a very debonair swathe in a white suit in 1980s Manchester as the exhibitions curator at the Whitworth. He has been loyal and generous down the years to the gallery and the collection, and he thought Pauline Karpidas, raised in Manchester, might like to meet the new woman running the Whitworth. It deserves the cliché, 'the beginning of a beautiful friendship'.

As Gregor Muir observes in his essay, it is a long journey from rainy Hoxton to Hydra. It felt an even longer one from Manchester to a renowned art world gathering on a Greek island. Yet the two are permanently linked through Pauline's generosity. Her motivation for The Hydra Workshop came from wanting to share her collection, and the artists she is interested in, with the people who live and visit the island she has made her summer home. Pauline's now long-standing support of the Whitworth comes from the Karpidas Foundation's desire to allow the Manchester public, most especially young people, to see the very best contemporary art as part of their daily experience in the city. The Karpidas works that hang in the gallery and Johnnie Shand Kydd's extraordinary, intimate record of 18 years of the art world in holiday mode, give the Whitworth and the people of Manchester a renewed and exciting relationship with the contemporary art world.

What is at the core of this, as all the participants in the Hydra weekend attest, is conviviality and hospitality. My own arrival on Hydra was accompanied by the fear that I would know no one and would stand out as a pale skinned Northerner, against the more beautiful polish of the art crowd. The welcome from two Paulines (Karpidas and Daly) and Sadie Coles put paid to these fears and then a chair and a G&T were offered by Johnnie Shand Kydd – the watcher and chronicler of the island weekend.

Johnnie takes his photographs mostly with a beautiful box camera. This means he is looking but not looking at his subjects. I think that this, more than anything, accounts for their deep candour. No one likes being stared at in their bikini and most artists are anyway very camera uncomfortable. Johnnie looks down, rather than toward, his subjects and in doing so, in friendship, he disarms them. It is also a mode of recording slow time. Johnnie's decision to document slowly and to let the real picture emerge over time (he never shared the year by year record with anyone other than Pauline) is a vital aspect of the atmosphere. This is not an Instagram sort of place. For in the speed and rush of the modern art world Hydra stands out as a place where people can have conversations and let an idea grow.

Showing Johnnie's photographs was a project born while we perched on loungers on Vlichos beach. Other elements of the new Whitworth would also not have come to fruition without the benefit of Hydra sunshine. A bronze snowman by Nate Lowman, now living permanently in Whitworth Park. Sarah Lucas's *Tits in Space*, wallpapering our upper gallery, Nico Vascellari's bronzes, *Bus de la Bum*, in the art garden – none of these would have found their way to Manchester without the particular encounters of the Hydra weekend.

As Gregor Muir notes, it would be easy to judge this an exclusive art world enclave. Our motivation for showing the photographs at the Whitworth comes from the opposite belief. The visitors to the Whitworth want to know who the faces behind the artworks are – they are interested and curious. There is a wonderful crossover between the artists in Johnnie's photographs and the artworks in the Whitworth collection. This shouldn't surprise us because Manchester is part of the art world too, and it has been since its 19th century philanthropists collected paintings and gifted them to the Whitworth. What is also shared most powerfully through these photographs is the generosity of spirit that has its roots in Pauline's Northern upbringing. She travelled a long way to Hydra, but never forgot where she came from.

Get them off the Island

Gregor Muir

*"There is little required from you other than an engagement with art
and guests, sunbathe, gossip and swim."*

Hydra itinerary since 2002
(same year as John Currin & Rachel Feinstein, The Hydra Workshops)

It was a very special moment in my life when I opened the front door of my then Shoreditch flat, overlooking Hoxton with its grey depressing skies, to find a breathless motorcycle courier with outstretched hand asking me to sign for a package. I padded back to my kitchen, ripped into its contents and puzzled over various slips of paper that left me wondering, what was a Flying Dolphin? Then it dawned on me – I was going to Hydra. Clearly, I owed much to London gallerist Sadie Coles, who was coordinating the trip, but behind all this was a very special someone, discreetly summoning a group of us for a long weekend in Greece.

I only knew of Pauline Karpidas in near mythical terms. Gary Hume had recently painted her portrait. Dealers often referred to her as the only collector in London who mattered. I observed how patrons of Tate, where I worked for a time, talked about Karpidas only to break into hysterical laughter in the midst of their whispers at something that was said, something unspeakable that might burn the ears off a saint. What was clear to me was that everyone loved Pauline. Anyone who'd met her had been won over by her personality. She was, as she later described herself to me, capricious. A Grande Dame with an appreciation of art rooted to her very core. To the younger generation, she was also one of us. We liked Pauline, her smile – her dark elegance. As for where we were going, Spiros, Athens, I had no idea having never been to Greece before.

*"It's really not a good idea to pet unattended donkeys, especially those tied up off
the port in the town and surrounding villages. Not all of them are used to being
touched by strange people, though they are perfectly content to let you pass
unmolested."*

http://www.hydraislandgreece.com/donkey-etiquette/

The waters around Hydra are what define it, piercing its rocky shoreline to make way for a port flanked by a modest sprawl of white and terracotta buildings. Chilled marble underfoot, the smoothed quayside stones swoop past the tinkling of moored boats and the long blustery tarpaulins hauled out to shield bar dwellers from the midday sun. To the left or right of the marina, the Saronic Gulf awaits in creaking cicada-filled groves. I like to think there are no mosquitoes on Hydra, just the sound of lapping water.

When Hydra started, it was a fairly small affair. A few drunken YBAs throwing themselves into the sea before returning that evening to a tiny restaurant tucked behind the harbour where, in hushed tones, word went round that Lauren Hutton was sat at a table nearby, and so she was! So many memories, but to pick one out, picture if you will Cerith Wyn Evans – immaculately dressed as ever – parading around the waterfront in a pair of shorts collaged with photographic prints of smiling dogs, only the one positioned right at the crotch holds a long white upright bone in its mouth.

Hydra then was not Hydra as it is now. I'm talking about a decade or so ago, with its wandering hippy harbour masters and a residue of Leonard Cohen's transcendental songs caught within the vacuum of this car-less idyll – a haven for retired mercenaries. Opposing this more romantic view, 'Volare', that tedious anthem of the southern European package holiday, once emanated from family restaurants as plates were smashed in celebration of the night's end. I also recall tourist stores adorned with pom-pom-like sponges offering lewd playing cards and toy cats that, when handled, seemed to be rather unnervingly made from cat – no doubt the fate of the feral moggies that flopped around the clock tower at noon.

From a small cluster around the table of a late-night bar, the party grew and grew until one year Hydra's voluminous expansion was marked by a flotilla of yachts descending on Richard Prince's opening at The Hydra Workshops, followed by an outdoor dinner, as I recall, for around three hundred people, possibly more.

Times have changed. I've stopped pointing out where Disco Heaven used to be – once a magnet for late-night drinkers, it was perched on a crest overlooking the harbour and is now a gated residence. In the face of glacial upward mobility, the Hydranetta Bar remains a constant and becomes something of a good friend over the long weekend. It feels like the bar at The World's End, a call for last orders just as the boutiques and restaurants that cup the port give way to solitary pathways and a gorgeous sort of nothingness. Having trekked all day from London and arriving in darkness, Hydranetta works its magic like an Aegean siren. Venturing down the cliffside to a long terrace with round tables served by a hut-like bar, it becomes all too tempting to leap into the baptismal waters below – deep as humanly possible. To emerge from the sea, hauling oneself onto a sodden concrete landing, exhausted, among friends, represents a moment of pure bliss.

So many artists would come to install their shows in The Hydra Workshops, with its distinctive, lumpy whitewashed walls. Over the years, it's where I met Frank Benson, Carroll Dunham, Nate Lowman, and Wilhelm and Anka Sasnal. It's where I continue to reconnect with international curators who, increasingly seem to use Hydra as a form of Annual General Meeting. Only in Hydra have I found myself treading water suspended in the wake of distant speed boats,

conversing with fellow bobbing apples – such as Gagosian's Robin Vousden, White Cube's Graham Steele and New York dealer Michelle Maccarone – as though this were all perfectly normal. Meanwhile, way over there on the beach, the annual gathering of gallerist Pauline Daly, photographer Johnnie Shand Kydd and theatre designer Christopher Woods, lounging on beach chairs at precisely the same spot they've occupied for several years, is nothing short of reassuring. At lunchtime, people make their way to a nearby restaurant and discuss things like fish.

> *"Well, here we are, at the taverna, where he ate for the first time all day (underwater fishing being conducive to fasting): a dish brought to him by his 12-year-old son – white beans with short macaroni, keftedes and hard-boiled eggs. And as any Greek would, despite how hungry he must have been he invited me to share his meal."*
> Mythology & Meatballs: A Greek Island Diary/Cookbook By Daniel Spoerri, 1982

Granted there will be critics of much of what is written here. I understand this may all sound excessive and provide further evidence of the increasingly lavish lifestyles being eked out by those who inhabit the contemporary art world. Equally, I might understand anyone who felt excluded by the cliquishness of it all. Nevertheless I'd like to thank Pauline Karpidas for getting me out of my hole, sticking me on a plane and bringing me to a place in the sun where I would learn so much from meeting artists, curators and gallerists in an environment that is utterly conducive to discussion, learning and exchange. Hydra will always remain a brilliant and generous offer and what Pauline would pilot here has given back so much to so many, including the local islanders with whom Pauline has been a regular feature having lived in Greece for over forty years.

Since that first knock at my door, I have continued to visit Hydra, on and off, and in doing so have found myself increasingly familiar with the island's mesmerising beauty, especially as one heads over the cliff tops down winding dirt tracks to Kamini beach. However, in all this time, it only recently occurred to me what was really being gifted here. Pauline didn't just give everyone a much-needed holiday – she gave us an island.

Hydra
Louisa Buck

"Hydra is a rock which rises out of the sea like a loaf of petrified bread. It is the bread turned to stone which the artist receives as reward for his labours when he first catches sight of the promised land."

Henry Miller, *The Colossus of Maroussi*, 1941

Of all the Greek islands, there's something special about Hydra. Rising out of the Aegean in Greece's Saronic Gulf, this small craggy island has a strikingly austere beauty, a ban on motorized transport and a long history as a creative crucible. Henry Miller was struck by Hydra's "purity" and "wild and naked perfection" when he came in 1939 to stay in the ancestral home of the prominent Greek artist Nikos Hadjikriakos-Ghikas; whose particularly Hellenic brand of Cubism was in turn influenced by the stark geometry of the white and blue houses stacked around Hydra's harbour. Sophia Loren filmed her first English-speaking movie, *Boy on a Dolphin*, on the island in 1957 and Hydra was also the location for Melina Mercouri's 1962 film *Phaedra*, made with her husband Jules Dassin and co-starring Antony Perkins.

Leonard Cohen also helped to put Hydra even more firmly on the cultural map when in 1960 he purchased a whitewashed town house above the harbour with a $1,500 bequest from his recently deceased grandmother which, despite recent financial tribulations, he still owns. American abstract painter Brice Marden is also another staunch Hydra devotee since he first arrived in the early 70s: his family now own two houses on the island and he continues to visit frequently and make work here.

Stringent planning regulations and the fact that you can only get around by boat, foot or donkey have ensured that Hydra remains a pristine refuge from the clamour of the 21st century. Yet it has also managed to avoid being trapped in a nostalgic time warp. For a quietly influential and highly hospitable initiative by another of the island's long- term aficionados has more recently been reinvigorating Hydra's role as a cultural catalyst and source of inspiration. For the past sixteen years the collector and patron Pauline Karpidas – who has made Greece her home for over half a century – has worked with the gallerist Sadie Coles and more recently also with her son Panos, to bring some the most significant members of the international art world to this remote spot by organizing an extraordinary series of annual exhibitions in The Hydra Workshops, a former boat repairers on the island's harbour waterfront.

Artists invited to show in this modest but generously proportioned space, with its raftered roof, bulbous whitewashed stone walls and worn flagstones, have included established names as well as those still at the beginning of their careers. These span from Christopher Wool, who exhibited in 1998, and Richard Prince, who showed some of his *Publicity* series in 2003, to young American painter Ryan Sullivan, who had his second-ever solo show in Hydra Workshops in 2013. Hydra Workshops may be distinctive in appearance but it is also surprisingly flexible: it has accommodated Tracey Emin, Sarah Lucas, Paul Noble and Gary Hume who in 1997 were part of a fifteen-strong multimedia young British artist show entitled *Package Holiday*, while just over a decade later, in 2008, American Carroll Dunham transformed its stony chamber into a limpid woodland glade with his recent series of paintings of trees. Newly-married artists John Currin and Rachel Feinstein called their first joint exhibition of his paintings and her sculpture in 2002 *The Honeymooners*; and in 2005 Swiss artist Urs Fischer made parts of his show in situ using chairs and tables from nearby Tassos café. Nate Lowman's work also responded directly to the specific context of Hydra by lining the Workshops' walls with a gregarious crowd of painted portraits based on Johnnie Shand Kydd's photographs of the extensive cast of guests who come every year to celebrate the latest exhibition and who form such an intrinsic part of the Hydra experience.

For the extraordinary generosity that Pauline Karpidas affords to the artists – no instructions, no stipulations and a dedicated publication to commemorate each exhibition – also extends to their friends and art world associates, who are also invited to stay in hotels throughout Hydra for the first weekend of the show. The only request is that everyone attends the exhibition opening on the Saturday night. This frenetic two day mass gathering of overlapping art clans in which a shifting constellation of exhibiting artists, their friends and family come together with a nucleus of regular invitees on beaches, boats and in bars has become an institution in its own right. Parties and social events abound in the art world, but the Hydra weekend is a unique chance for all its different elements to spend time together in stunning surroundings and without any obligation or agenda.

The result is a special spirit of joyous freedom which shines through Johnnie Shand Kydd's vivid and evocative photographs and informs the statements gathered here from just a few of those who have been touched by their time on Hydra. For Pauline Karpidas' ongoing act of hospitality is an act of patronage inextricably intertwined with, and as important as, the exhibitions at its centre, and it has had a crucial impact not only on the island of Hydra but on the art world at large.

Pauline Karpidas:

I first came to Hydra in the early 60s. I was in Athens for a wedding and had a couple of days spare and so I decided to go to the nearby islands. I got on the ferry and Poros was nice and Aegina was nice but then suddenly I come around this corner and there were these rocks and this unbelievable island that had nothing to do with Poros or Aegina! I get out and I see all these wonderful old, old men sitting on the harbour side, knitting their fishing nets and speaking to me in Greek as – because I am very dark – they thought as I was a Greek; and I was sitting down by them and not understanding a word and looking around me and thinking, Oh my God, isn't this wonderful!

I opened a boutique in Athens but I would always go back to Hydra and swim off the rocks and then later on I would often come with Dinos, my late husband. Being an engineer he'd refurbished all the harbours after the war and he loved this island: it was still very Oriental, they would dance the *bouzouki* and sing all these Greek songs and you would see these ladies drenched in their black mourning gowns who would only come down to potter around the port in the late afternoon and early evening. Hydra was a very private island, the Voulgaris family and the Boudouris family and the other big families who had become dominant on Hydra all had these beautiful traditional homes, lined with paintings. The artist Ghikas had a house here and also Jannis Kounellis in my time. My husband was a very dear friend of Melina Mercouri and I remember in the early 80s he, Melina, her husband Jules Dassin and Alexander Iolas were all talking about the film that she had made on Hydra [*Phaedra*, 1962] and I said, "Oh, I do love Hydra, it's my place – I'm sure I will end up there!" and she said, "my darling this is where you will be – it is the most poetic island." and then Alexander said, "yes, you have to do something for Hydra!" But I never thought of it at the time.

Then everything just fell into place like stepping stones. A friend of Dinos had this little tourist shop in the harbour and he said, "look, I know you want something, why don't you buy this?" So we bought it, and although it was in need of repair, it was a beautiful space with a fabulous mezzanine that went on forever, where they used to restore the wooden *kaiki* fishing boats. I got David Gill and Mattia Bonetti to make this wonderful wooden furniture, and our first exhibition was of Mattia's gorgeous black and white ceramic temples which we showed with Grayson Perry in 1996 – and that was the first show of the Hydra Workshop. I'd been coming backwards and forwards to London and then the next year I met Sadie, and that's how it all really started.

To bring people together and to give people enjoyment for three days of the year is one of the most satisfying things, and also to be able to represent the artist and try to let them see what can happen with their vision. It's been an amazing to think of some of the great artists who have been here. But it's about coming together and being part of life and giving something back. We are very fortunate that we can do this and be able to meet these wonderful people who come here and bring their energy. There's no agenda here: it's not about buying, it's not about selling, it's about coming together on this beautiful island which I have been visiting during the fifty years I have lived in Greece, and all those anecdotes that we've all shared over the years and all those wonderful things that will make another book one day…

Sadie Coles:

Pauline was one of the first collectors who supported my opening shows in 1997. She immediately bought a painting by John Currin and a self-portrait by Sarah Lucas. These conversations led to a discussion about a YBA group exhibition in her former boat repair shop in Hydra port and we selected a group of fifteen artists from her collection for an exhibition called *Package Holiday*. A key ingredient of what was to become an annual event was the invitation to the exhibiting artists and a selection of curators, writers and other enthusiasts to come to Hydra for a long weekend at Pauline's expense for a private celebration of contemporary art and the very special island of Hydra. Since then there have been solo and group shows, actual commissions and art made specifically to reflect the context or the Karpidas patronage and taste – but the holiday premise has remained intact. Over the years there have been many friendships formed between artists, curators, collectors, art dealers and writers, and exhibitions, texts, new representation, sales, friendships, romances, Greek house acquisitions and babies have all gestated during the Karpidas weekend. For Pauline and Panos I imagine it is as much the chance to share Greece and Hydra as it is to actually live with, and learn from, the art they have acquired. For those of us lucky enough to be along for the ride, it is a refreshing return to a genuine, involved, living patronage: a golden ticket.

Paul Noble:
(Hydra Workshop: *Package Holiday* 1997)

Who was there? Don Brown, Tracey Emin, Angus Fairhurst, Sarah Lucas, Georgina Starr, Nicola Tyson, Gillian Wearing, Michael Landy, Abigail Lane and Anya Gallaccio. I knew Tracey, Sarah, Gillian and Michael. When I arrived in Hydra harbour I saw donkeys with crates of art on their backs. Somehow I didn't have a penny. The little that I was able to withdraw had just got me to the island. Sadie gave me £90! 'Too much'. I had to spend it immediately. I went to the nearest harbour touristic shop and bought every inflatable. Money well spent. One became Johnnie's floating tripod for out-at-sea shots. I was sharing a room with Johnnie. This was when I learnt that underpants could be made from material other than cotton – PINK SILK! The day was: breakfast, fruit, yoghurt and honey, on the harbour front. Then swimming. Then lunch. Then swimming. Then slobbing. Food? Last swim. After the last swim of the day and the sun had set the moon began its ascent into the sky. It came from out of the ground and climbed (or was it pushed?) up the left hand side of the distant equilateral mountain until it had rolled all the way to the top, by which time it had acquired enough momentum to make its way up into the night without further help. This moon told us "Now is the time to ascend to Disco Heaven". Disco Heaven, Hydra's No.1 dance spot, up lots of steps, where I made a pact (with Angus and Don) to dance as badly as possible, apologies to the DJ. What else? Sarah got glued, face down, to the beautifully shiny warm slabs of the harbour promenade. She was unmovable, pinned to the floor by alcoholic gravity and night-time stone love. Gillian and Michael wore coats buttoned up throughout. After, when I got home, I was so spent I slept through a dawn raid by Interpol who arrested my neighbours for murder. I realised that I missed Georgina.

Anne Collier:
(Hydra Workshop 2014)

I'd visited Hydra once before – when my friend Nate Lowman presented his work at the Hydra Workshop – so I was familiar with the idiosyncratic nature of the space and also its spectacular harbor-front setting. The Hydra Workshop integrates art into the everyday life of the town in a way that makes absolute sense. Pauline Karpidas and Sadie Coles have created a truly unique context for artists. It was really interesting to see my work – which is often very formal – in such an informal and ultimately relaxed environment, where passersby might wander in on their way to the beach or as they headed out to dinner at night. I enjoyed that juxtaposition. It's a very different experience to how we typically encounter art. Normally I'm stressed out at my own openings – often to the point of distraction – but at Hydra I had the best time!

Beatrix Ruf:
(Director, Stedelijk Museum, Amsterdam)

When the email comes it is always a big excitement to find out who is going to be coming this year. The way in which the hospitality is extended to an island, to a town, and the combination of people who spend time together is very, very particular. It is not just that someone invites you to an island and you get to spend some free time there: what is particularly interesting is the intensity of that weekend and the fact that there is this exhibition and the way in which the context of the artist who is showing each year is always re-arranging this group. The range of artists who show at the Workshop reflects the way in which Pauline lives with contemporary art and is always looking at young artists, and so once a year we get to see what she is thinking about! Then the space itself is also very generous, given the architecture of Hydra, and it is very nice to wonder what happens when we are not all there, what a different life it has.

Nicholas Cullinan:
(Director of the National Portrait Gallery)

I met Pauline Karpidas seven years ago when I first started work at Tate Modern. I think we bonded over a sneaky cigarette and the fact that we were both from the north of England. I've been lucky enough to go to Hydra several times since then, which has been such an education in several ways. It's not just where I've seen some great exhibitions by each of the artists selected and also where I've met a fascinating and lively group of artists, collectors, curators and dealers, but more importantly, it's given me a chance to get to know them properly and form friendships. Hydra is an incredibly generous event to organize (for which thanks also have to go to the sterling work of Sadie Coles Gallery), not just in the obvious sense, but in the way it brings people together and gives them time to get to know one another. Collectors are ten-a penny these days, but patrons are rare and that is what Pauline is.

Nate Lowman:
(Hydra Workshop 2009)

I first went to Hydra, having been brought by a girlfriend, in 2005. It was as far as I'd ever been away from home, and bore little resemblance to any place I'd been before. The lack of motor vehicles enabled a profound silence that gave way to the intense chorus of crickets rubbing their little legs together in the heat. It was all very surreal, yet cheery; the port full of strangers on holiday, Greek donkey men, hundreds of stray cats, and endless horiatiki.

Being 26 and having never really been on 'holiday' as an adult, things were already feeling sideways on this charming island when I looked up and saw my friends from New York, Clarissa Dalrymple and Gavin Brown, sitting down for a drink at the table next to mine. It turns out they were the guests of Pauline Karpidas, a woman who commissions an artist or group of artists every year to exhibit in a (modest by contemporary standards, but still rather grand) gallery she owns in the port. That year the artist was Urs Fisher.

Coincidentally, Clarissa had persuaded Pauline to purchase one or two of my paintings earlier that very summer at the Basel art fair. She introduced me to Pauline, who was sweet and magnetic, and we've remained close ever since. Pauline invited me to exhibit at Hydra's workshop in 2009. By then I had been to Hydra three times, and grown friendly with the cast of characters who are invited as guests to these annual exhibitions. The organization of both the social and artistic aspects of the exhibitions are handled by the ever graceful Sadie Coles. When it was my turn to make an exhibition, she liaised with me over the course of a year leading up to the show.

Generously, the commission was open ended: I was to make whatever I pleased in return for a lump sum. As the exhibition on Hydra is 'destination' based, I felt compelled to make something site-specific with regards to content and installation. As someone who works primarily in painting, this is a bit of a challenge. I decided to address the situation as directly as possible by asking for a list of the invited guests and painting each person's portrait. Many of the guests return year after year, and the event is documented each time by Johnnie Shand Kydd. I told Johnnie about my idea and asked him if I could have access to his Hydra archive. We met in London, where he showed me box after box of photos that chronicled the annual exhibition. I ended up making many, if not most, of my portraits using images culled directly from his contact sheets. Johnnie was a generous collaborator, and shared his materials freely with me. I've been to Hydra 9 times.

Ryan Sullivan:
(Hydra Workshop 2013)

In this current climate where galleries are getting bigger and bigger and everything is seen globally and documented up the wazoo, it's actually a relief to do an intimate show in a small space, and to experiment with how things are going to look together. It was challenging to install because the paintings I was showing already had a lot of texture in them, and I was daunted by the idea of putting them on the gallery's stone walls, but in the end it worked: the wall sort of disappeared, and the paintings were all able to talk to each other. I think it's very generous to create this environment in the way that Pauline does. She never interfered, and there were no expectations or restrictions on me. It was like, let's just take this space and do something and experiment with it... and that's pretty uncommon in my experience. And there are no expectations for the guests, either. Everyone just goes there, shows up, and whatever happens is what happens, and that's actually not so different from being the artist who is making the show.

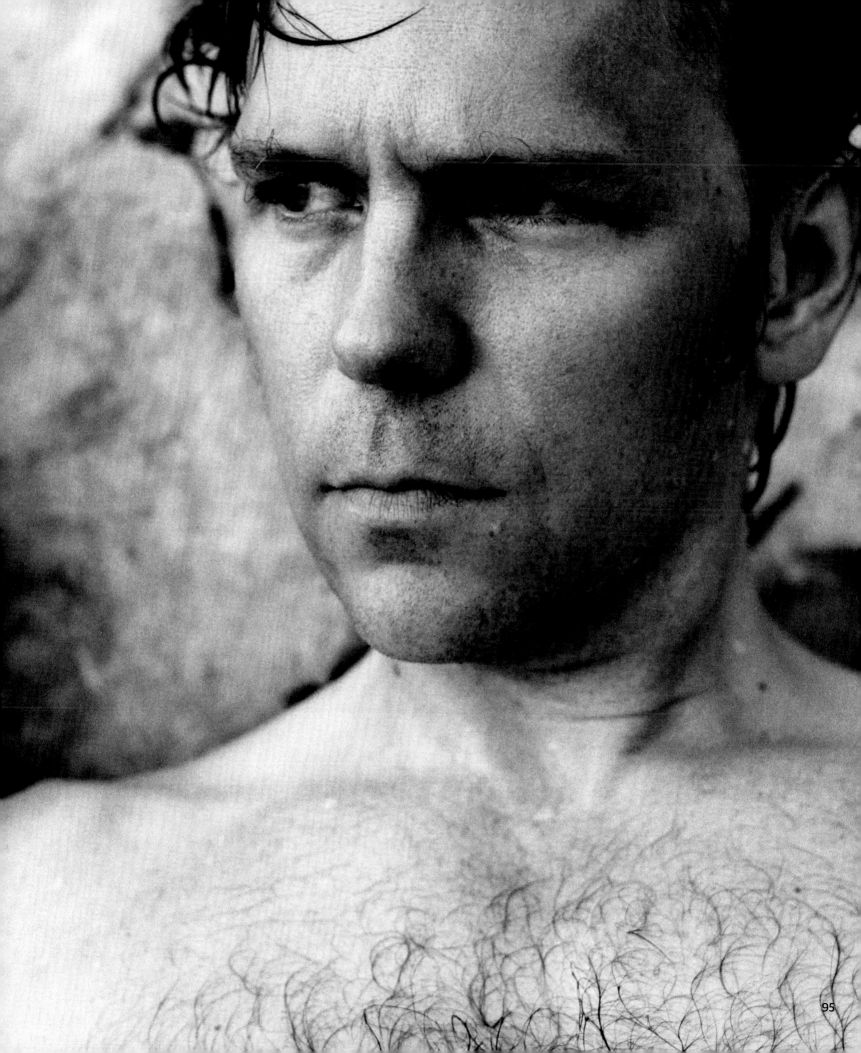

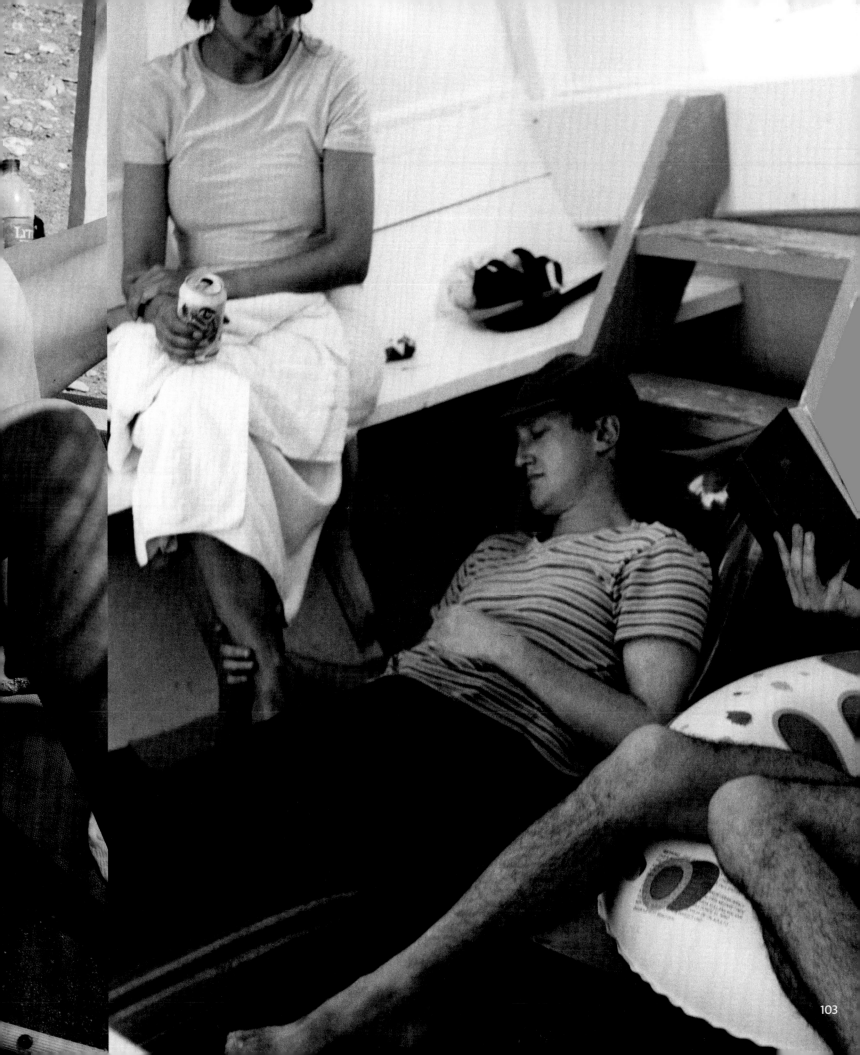

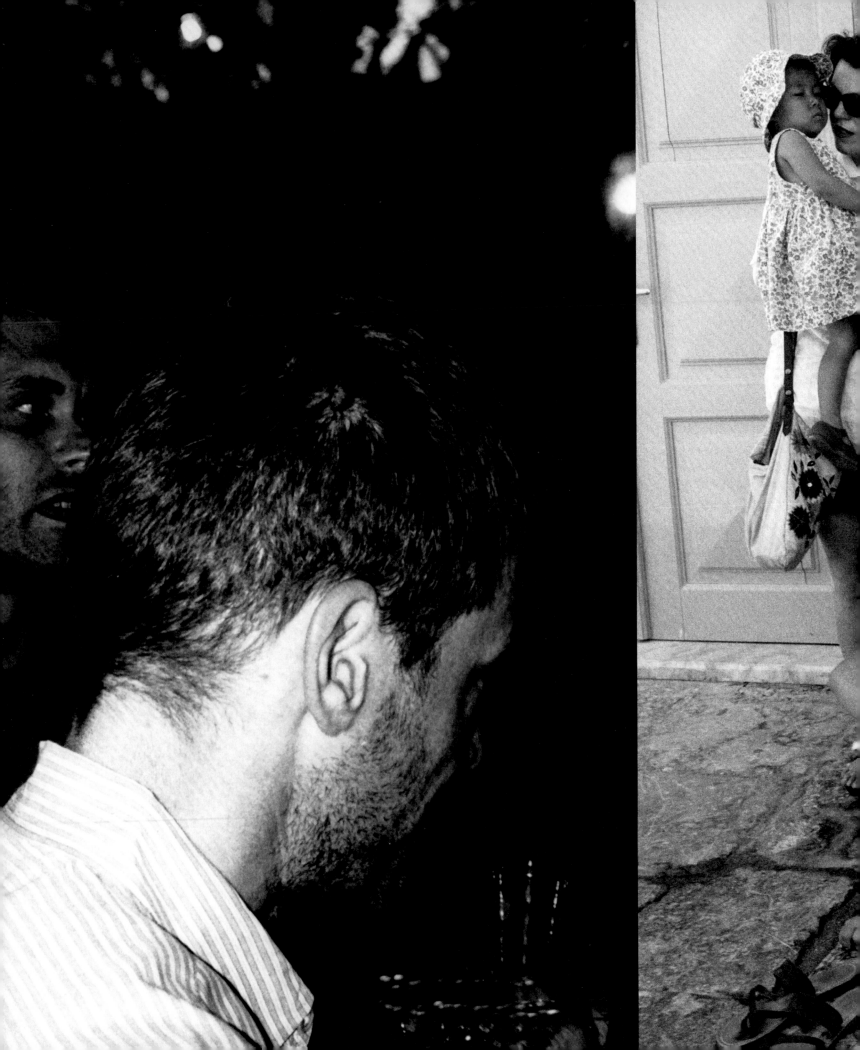